MW01231000

Poetry for the Battered Soul

Michelle Duggins

Copyright © 2017 Michelle Duggins

All rights reserved.

ISBN:1493783432
ISBN-13:978-1493783434

DEDICATION

For every woman out there who feel that they must fight a battle of abuse alone...? I am here to let you know that you are not alone! For I know what it feels like to be in the battle not just for your life, but for your sanity as well, and your will and desire to walk away from a world of darkness when everything you say and do is used against you, by your love one, whom I had the pleasure of calling my love one the enemy...

Ladies I am not there to physically remove you from your situation but I do encourage you to seek help, please don't feel ashamed or embarrassed believe me your life is in danger. You may not see it or you may refuse to see it, because he blinds you with love and affection when he knows that he had done wrong! Ladies this is a cycle BE AWARE!

Ladies letting go and letting God is how I made it through, finding that spiritual live that is inside of me, helped me become stronger. Giving it to God is your deliverance from your world of darkness...

Ladies I pray that God's heavenly light will shine through the darkest hours in your life and lead you through your trials and tribulations. AMEN

Michelle Duggins

CONTENTS

ACKNOWLEDGMENTS

I would like to say thank you to my loving children. You all are my inspiration when I was going through the good and bad. Daniel, James and Victoria, thank you and I love each of you dearly.

I would like to thank you my best friends from the Long Island. Lisa, Stephanie, Vivian and Stacey, if it wasn't for the friendship that we all shared where would we be? We all hung together and were never one without the other, but as the years past and life stepped in, we all had certain directions to go and life trials and tribulation to face. So, here I am once again to say thank you, thank you God for all of our paths crossing and becoming one.

Special thanks to my mother and aunt you are special in my life, love you.

To my Brother, gone to soon!. I love you and you are special to me, you were the bridge that connected two states together, which kept lines open. Love you dearly.

.

1 BUTTERFLY

I want to lift my eyes up to the sky and feel pain no more.

I want to soar with the wind and live forever more

I want to be freed of bondage that held me down- verbal abuse, hate, jealous, deceit, greed and physical violence.

My soul has gathered strength from am almighty source,

A source which is greater than you and I, a source which helped me to see not in the dark but within the light!

A source that has shown me love and peace, a source that said "My child you will no longer weep or feel man's hand upon your body.

This source I speak of is grater then you and I, this source that I speak of it my heavenly father and my deliver of peace".

I am that butterfly who flies high above all things that has shackled me and held me down. But now my chains have been broken!

I am that butterfly that has lifted her eyes towards the sky and soared were no man or woman has gone before.

My journeys, my trials and my tribulations.

I am that butterfly, which represents the day of resurrection! The day which is the new beginning within my life?

Jesus said, "I tell you: Love your enemies and pray for those who persecute you, that you may be sons of your father and heaven".

Matthew 5:44-45 (NIV)

2 TWISTED

My life is twisted upside down, full of lies, deceit, and physical abuse, and not to mention his controlling arguing ways. What happened to my life? Where did all my family and friends go? No hellos how are you, or I was thinking about you!

All I see are frowns, like I asked for this to happen to me. My dear Lord why is this happening to me? Why is my life twisted Upside down?

My days and nights are long in this house, wondering if I am doing things right. Why must I second guest myself? I used to be strong and full of fight, but now I'm not sure, I don't want to make him explode.

What a twisted life I live, why don't I just get up and leave? I found excuses of why not to leave, he loves me, he had bad day, I'm sorry I Didn't mean to do that, it was your fault, you asked for it. Well enough already

I said to myself, until one day I said enough is enough and called on my Lord for guidance and help.

I waited and I prayed until one day God intervened, and said to me, "My child I was with you every day, you never called on me to help you make it through the day".

"My child he said I heard your cries, I was preparing for you a stronger and solid ground".

My lord saved me from a twisted upside down life, and placed me on solid ground and placed me on a path, were people that I meet along the way were able to help me.

Each and everyday I grew stronger in the Lord and keep the faith. Now on this day that I write this for you, I am glad to say I am saved, now what about you?

"Do not fear, for I am with you: do not be dismayed for I am your God. I will strengthen you and help you; I will uphold you with my righteous right hand".

Isaiah 41:10 (NIV)

3 REFLECTION IN THE MIRROR

When you look in the mirror, what do you see? Do you look in the mirror and see the image of yourself or a reflection of who you would like to be?

When you look in the mirror, what do you see? Do you see fame and fortune, or do you see calamity and despair?

When you look in the mirror, what do you see? Do you see the love that God has for you, or do you see hate that society has embedded in your head? When you look in the mirror tell me what do you see?

Look deep within your soul and tell me are you all that you can truly be? " Step away from the mirror and face reality, no more busted lips, no more swollen face or eyes shut".

"Girl, you are a wonder, a gift from God, how dear you not stand strong and face the crowd."

"Praise be to the God and Father of our Lord Jesus Christ, the Father of compassion and the God of all comfort, who comforts us in all our troubles, with the comfort we ourselves have received from God".

2 Corinthians 1: 3-4 (NIV)

4 A RAY OF LOVE

A ray of hope, a ray of joy, a ray of love, a ray of sunlight that flickers through my window shades.

 As I raise my head from my pillow upon which it rest, awaking from a night of slumber.

Face swollen! Eyes shut! All this by the man I loved.

 A ray of joy! A ray of love!

A ray of sunlight, that flickers through my window shades.

Through all the pain, the misery and lies, I still failed to realize, that the love I was searching for was here all of the time.

Through a ray of hope through a ray of joy, through a ray of sunlight that flicker through my window shades.

It was here all the time, the love that I desired through the hope of it all and the joy and the rays of light. That spiritual love was there the whole time.

"The Lord is close to the brokenhearted and saves those who are crushed in spirit".   Psalm 34:18 (NIV)

5 TENDER ROSE

I am a beautiful flower which stands tall and strong, and that is due to the strong foundation which is rooted in the ground.

The roots provide all the strength that I need, because it is embedded deep within the soil, which I feel represents me standing tall.

Now as we travel to the top, Oh! What a sight to behold, the beauty of the petals soft and delicate as it may be. It truly is a sight to see.

I am like a tender rose, what a beauty to behold. When I feel that I am in danger, I have learned to stand strong and to be resilient against the fight.

Your words blow right pass me, like it blows past the petals in the wind.

My body may bend and shake with the strongest gust of wind, but I must say look at me I'm still standing.

The thorns represent the skin that covers me; it helps to protect my most precious part which is inside of me and that is my heart.

You see ladies, we are like a tender rose we have a strong foundation which starts with the roots and the stem represents our bodies. The petals represent our body and our love.

When the flower opens, it's just as beautiful on the inside as well as the outside.

Remember when people handle you make sure it's with respect and love, because any roughness will leave you bruised just like a rose whose petals turn brown, scarred and old when it is handled in a rough manner.

"The Lord will guide you always; he will satisfy your needs in a sun scorched land and will strengthen your frame. You will be like a well-watered garden, like a spring whose waters never fail". Isaiah 58:11 (NIV)

6 TERMINATED

I've given you so much of my time, trust, dedication and even shared a smile or two. I worked seven days a week from sun up until sun down.

I dealt with other people rudeness including yours as well. I dealt with foolishness and racism too!

Yes! At times it demoralized my spirit and my trust that I had towards others. Yes! You were the boss! you were given a title, and you did not show any compassion and or understanding, because your workers saved your back. Or should I say had your back!

If you only knew how I felt. I cried inside, not wanting you to see , how vulnerable I could be.

Don't get it twisted, I did not cry because of what you said to me. I cried for how you spoke to others and try to devalue me!

But despite it all I gave you my best. I respected the ground you walked on, because I thought it was best!

Here you come in my life to tell me I'm terminated, the one who stayed late hours, because no one else would, me, the lady who ran around making sure everything was in order, me the lady who wore so many hats.

You come to tell me that I am no long needed. That I am Terminated!

"Hell, I even lied for you to protect your hide, what a shock to the system

after all that I had given".

Not once did you ask how I was feeling, you never knew what I was thinking, that in my mind, I was saying "this is a mistake".

I kept my composure and gathered my things and with a smile on my face, said thank you for everything, God bless and take care.

Feeling some kind of way, I sat in my car; I sat there for a while and cried oh God!

It took a while but comfort came, when sitting by myself and hearing God say, "I am your creator listen to me, do as I say and your life my child will never be the same".

Ladies, Have you ever been terminated by a spouse, a friend, a family member, or even a job?

If so, please hold tight, be strong and believe that God will lift you up and he will carry you through the storm.

Your faith and patience will pay off in the end; God will deliver you from your heartaches and sin.

Your rewards and riches shall be great!

"Whatever you do, work at it with all your heart, as working for the Lord, not for men, since you know that you will receive an inheritance from the Lord as a reward. It is the Lord Christ you are serving".

Colossians 3:23-24 (NIV)

7 HURT

Baby you said you loved me, don't you remember?

Just yesterday we made plans on being together forever, as we lay upon the grass, and glazed upon the clouds that gently past us by.

But as night fell, you started to change; you became an enemy, which I dared not to stare. One blink, one breath, I would be down the stairs.

Why do I love you so? When all you do is belittle me and hit me.

You used to be so kind, considered and patient too. All I see now is the devil in you! Oh, how the pain rises from within, the bruises, the cuts and even demoralization too!

"I want out of this world of pain; I need a knight and shining armor, to rescue me from a world of heartache and pain". I'm scared and hurt and feel all alone, someone, anyone, don't you hear my calls?

The windows are open, the yelling hasn't cease, the neighbors can hear me, but they won't even speak.

I fall on my knees, and yell, God please help me! I'm tired of being hurt and in pain, so come and save me!

Right then and there on my knees, I felt joy and peace come over me. I stood up tall, my head up high, as tears flowed down from my eyes.

I felt all hurt and pain dissolve from within, and it was replaced, with joy in knowing that my day has come.

"I've been saved and released from the strong hold that the enemy had on me, no more hurt and no more pain".

God is good, the whole time he's been with me, he was my comforter, my doctor, my friend, and yes indeed he was the one carrying me.

"That knight and shining armor, it was him too! And in the end he became my deliver and my prince of peace, yes, he is my savior too."

"You turned my wailing into dancing; you removed my sackcloth and clothed me with joy, that my heart may sing to you and not to be silent. O Lord, I will give you thanks forever".

Psalms 30: 11-12 (NIV)

8 I MISS ME

I miss me, my smile, my laugh, my soft gentle ways.

I miss me, my loving ways and my caring attitude towards others. I miss me, where have you gone?

I miss me, feeling the sunshine against my face and the wind blowing through my hair; I miss knowing that life is full of great opportunities and happiness.

I miss the things I did for myself, I miss loving myself for who I am and what I stand for.

Where did I go, who stole the real me? I fell in love with the man of my dreams, my night and shining armor, my prince and my protector.

Oh! How could this be? This man has threaten me. It must be the bad day he had at work or the guy that hit his car. Lord knows he would not hurt me!

I miss me, where did I go? I'm laying here in a hospital bed, hearing that I will never walk again, Oh my god! What happened to me? Where did I go? I'm missing me.

I am lost within this body and I can't get out, crying and screaming, for someone to let me out. My goodness! MY God! HE can't hear me!

He has beaten me and caused me pain. But in silence, I cried and made it easy for him. by telling him all these lies.

Jesus, I miss me and all I use to do, the wind in my hair, the smiles on my face, and hearing myself say Lord, I love you!

Just being able to run, walk and laugh, was something I loved to do, but now a man that I loved took it away from me!

He took my life, and silenced my world, He said he would never hurt me and that he loved me so much.

He promised to be by my side and to make sure that I was safe, loved and cared for.

Where did I go Lord? I miss me! I need you now more than ever Lord! Come and rescue me!

I miss me, I miss me, I miss me oh Lord! just to be able to laugh and run again, what a joy that would be.

Lord! If you are hearing me in this silent world of mind, I forgive him Lord! I forgive him for what he has done to me.

In order to move on and to leave this hospital bed, I must forgive him, and I ask that you bless me.

I must say good bye to a life I once knew, and say hello, to a new and improved me.

"The Lord will fight for you; you need only to be still"

Exodus 14:14 (NIV)

9 UNTOUCHED

I am walking through a world that is crumbling down around me.

Days are filled, with lies and regrets, along with words that tears at your heart.

We argue, we laugh and I cry alone at night, what in the world is wrong with this man?

For better or worse, are the vows that we shared, not knowing that your heart was planning a major farewell.

Before you leave, you feel that you must prove to me, that you are a man, by belittling me.

Calling me names, and even calling Jesus names that I will never say.

I said come let's pray let's keep God near, all you did was cursed his name. I'm tired and ready to go to bed he said. I stayed in the room, behind locked door.

I cried and I prayed, but I kept my faith, knowing that my God is a deliver and always right on time.

All the fear that I once had, the burden of working hard, and coming home, to a man I don't even know.

I was living with the enemy, can you believe it, he used to be a deacon in the church.

Close your eyes and lift your praises unto the Lord, he will hear your cries; he's right by your side.

Bow your head my child and rest your soul, for I am here, to protect you and to deliver peace unto you.

You will be untouched by those who are out to harm you.

I will always be there for you.

Rest my child, Rest my dear child, Rest.

Jesus said, "Come to me, all you who are weary and burdened, and I will give you rest. Take my yoke upon you and learn from me, for I am gentle and humble in heart, and you will find rest for your soul.   For my yoke is easy and my burden is light".

Matthew 11:28-30 (NIV)

10 YESTERDAY

Yesterday my soul was free living my life so care free.

Yesterday I prayed morning, noon and night.

Praising my lord, until the morning light,

Praising my lord, until the morning light.

Yesterday my life was almost taken by someone I Love.

Yesterday you came at me, so full of rage and anger.

Yesterday you came at me, so full of rage and anger.

Yesterday the enemy came knocking at the door, No, not for me, but for the love, that doesn't live here anymore.

No more yesterdays of feeling hurt or all alone.

No more yesterday's being a victim of someone else's Insecurity.

Yesterday's my soul was tired and battered, tired of being a punching bag.

Being a target of hate and despair, yes, my soul is tired and battered.

My soul was tired and battered, but through the pain of it all.

Through the trials, and tribulation of it all.

I carried the pain and hid the scars, and fell on my knees, and looked towards the sky.

I prayed and prayed, until, I fell asleep on the floor.

Yesterday I prayed until I fell asleep, today I awoke to find that I am fine.

No more bad yesterdays, no more battered soul.

No more being tired, No more weary nights or worried soul.

Praising my lord until the morning light.

Yesterday my soul was free, living my life so care free.

Praising my Lord.

Morning, noon and night.

The LORD is my strength and my shield; my heart trusts in him, and I am helped. MY heart leaps for joy and I will give thanks to him in song

Psalm 28

11. BATTERED

Mistreated, Misused and disregard like garbage. Why do you treat me like I'm not even your wife?

You go out and stay all night and lie by saying you worked through the night. Feeling down and all alone and sometimes feeling lost and like I don't belong. The man I married loved me so dearly, he wined and dined me and never misguided me. He even said how much he loved me and that he will never leave my side!

Here I am today my world of lovely bliss, turned into a dream of an unforgiven kiss, a kiss that poisoned not my mind, but yours my love. Do you remember the night you came home and accused me of sin?

When all along it was you on the fence, I spoke my mind on what I was feeling. While you got angry and started to flip...Oh! You say you don't remember, but look where you are at, a man who had everything, exquisite homes and cars, and a beautiful wife.

You exchanged it all for lust, infidelity and Lord knows what else. You say you didn't do it, you were too drunk to remember. You took your knife and cut me from ear to chin, then you beat me until my life seemed as if it was going to end, broken ribs and broken nose, all from a man who vowed to love me forever more.

Here I am Three years later, by the grace of God I survived and sitting before you, where you are serving time. I came to tell you my testimony and to let you know, that I gave God the glory and that he took the pain away.

My ex I forgive you, from the very night you tried to destroy me. I forgave myself for all that I put up with. I came to tell you this face to face, that I will continue to pray for you, as you make this your everlasting resting place.

You took my life away, as so you think, how can another man love me with a messed up face? I will tell you this much, God is so awesome, he blessed me with a wonderful man, he loves me for me. My scars and all.

So, as you serve life behind those prison walls, I will leave you with this Bible and pray that you will one day find the love and peace through Gods word.

Ladies you must remember that part of the healing process is forgiving the one that hurt you! You must let go of the feeling of hate in order to move on. Yes! It is hard, but take it day by day, put the effort forward and God will help you the rest of the way.

"Get rid of all bitterness, rage and anger, brawling and slander, along with every form of malice. Be kind and compassionate to one another, forgiving each other, just as in Christ God will forgive you"

Ephesians 4:31-32 (NIV)

ABOUT THE AUTHOR

Michelle is a single divorced mother of three children. Living in the state of South Carolina. After being a victim and now a survivor of domestic abuse. Michelle is following the word that God spoke unto her about being an advocate for women of domestic abuse.

Michelle loves writing, cooking for others and reading Gods word. You can also find Michelle assisting others with their business plans and ideas. Michelle is also a Published author of a children's book entitled Valley of The Flowers and she is in the book of anthologies for her poetry.

Michelle loves to attend church and loves to talk and spend time with her grandchildren.
Michelle is on a mission to grow her organization Flying High with Butterflies Women's Support Group.

If you would like to contact Michelle please email her at: jewelrydiva97@gmail.com